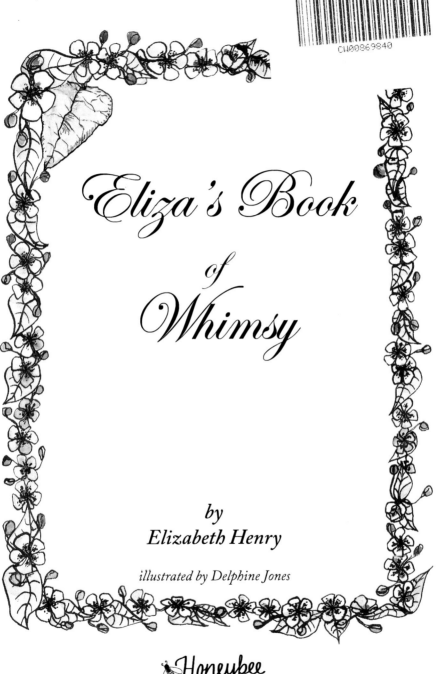

Eliza's Book

of

Whimsy

by
Elizabeth Henry

illustrated by Delphine Jones

Honeybee
Books

Published by Honeybee Books
Broadoak, Dorset
www.honeybeebooks.co.uk

Copyright © Elizabeth Henry 2016
Images Copyright © Delphine Jones 2016

Printed in the UK using paper from sustainable sources

ISBN: 978-1-910616-60-4
Website: www.elizabethhenry.co.uk
Email: info@elizabethhenry.co.uk

For my son, who's precious

The beach at Gyrn Goch, North Wales; inspiration for The Seashore.

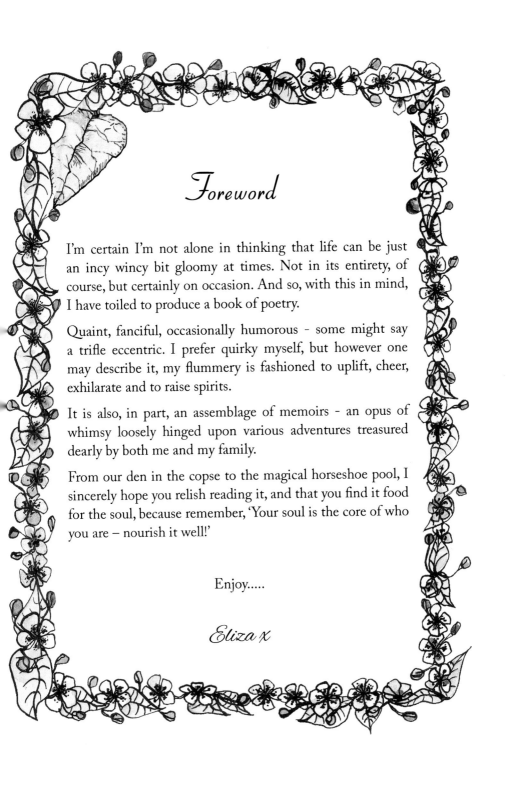

Foreword

I'm certain I'm not alone in thinking that life can be just an incy wincy bit gloomy at times. Not in its entirety, of course, but certainly on occasion. And so, with this in mind, I have toiled to produce a book of poetry.

Quaint, fanciful, occasionally humorous - some might say a trifle eccentric. I prefer quirky myself, but however one may describe it, my flummery is fashioned to uplift, cheer, exhilarate and to raise spirits.

It is also, in part, an assemblage of memoirs - an opus of whimsy loosely hinged upon various adventures treasured dearly by both me and my family.

From our den in the copse to the magical horseshoe pool, I sincerely hope you relish reading it, and that you find it food for the soul, because remember, 'Your soul is the core of who you are – nourish it well!'

Enjoy.....

Eliza x

Contents

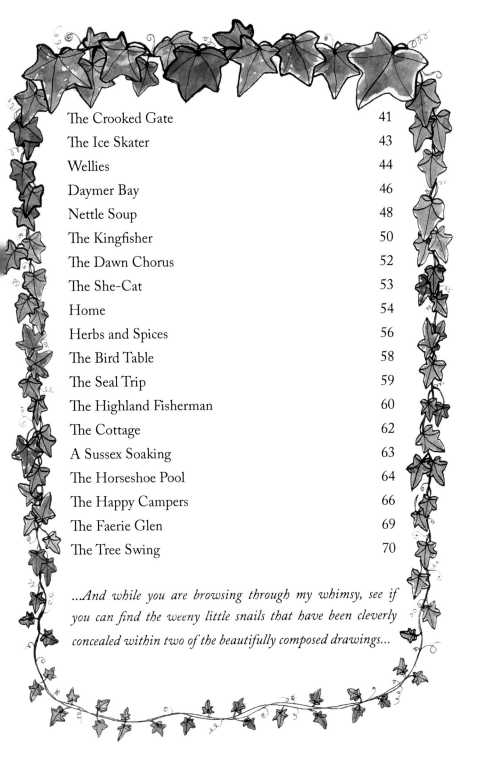

...And while you are browsing through my whimsy, see if you can find the weeny little snails that have been cleverly concealed within two of the beautifully composed drawings...

About the Poems

~

"Thank you, Billy Blackbird, from the bottom of my heart..."

My poetic pilgrimage began April last, whilst seated beneath a willow's weeping bough, just to the left of the vegetable patch. I was already an ardent reader and a dilettante writer, but like the unremarkable blackbird that roused me that day, I was a fledgling—a fledgling poet about to take flight.

I watched him, my garrulous friend, as he flitted and fleeted amongst a tangle of bramble close by, and as I sipped hot tea and breathed the sweetly scented spring air, I thought how endearing he was for such an unembellished bird. This set my mind whirring, and in a moment I'd scrawled a little rhyme in his honour—short but undeniably sweet.

Other poems swiftly followed, each and every one a far better verselet than my humble blackbird. Nonetheless, he had given me the nudge I needed, because by then, the fire inside me was vehement and with 'simple pleasures' as my stimulus, I proceeded to pen my first opus: a garland of whimsy, loosely hinging upon the many adventures treasured dearly by myself and my family.

Of course, the collection wouldn't look anywhere near as wonderful as it does without the acumen of Delphine, the book's illustrator. With nothing more than my waggish wordery, she has produced artwork that in itself is poetry—silent poetry through perfect painting.

enter

The Blackbird

Busy Billy Blackbird
Sits atop a twig.
He hasn't any colour
Just a hop, a skip, a jig.

He trills a merry birdsong
As he ventures on his way,
Oblivious to wily cats
Who think of him as prey.

As he darts betwixt the branches,
He always makes me smile,
So I stop my toil and digging,
And I listen for a while.

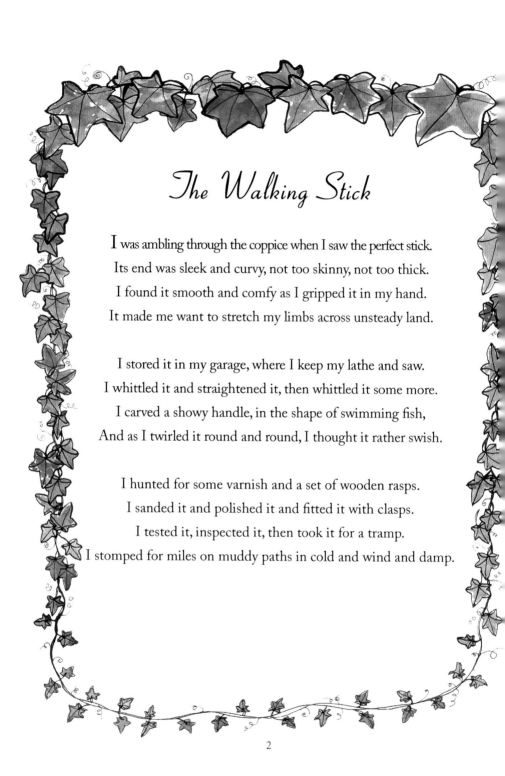

The Walking Stick

I was ambling through the coppice when I saw the perfect stick.
Its end was sleek and curvy, not too skinny, not too thick.
I found it smooth and comfy as I gripped it in my hand.
It made me want to stretch my limbs across unsteady land.

I stored it in my garage, where I keep my lathe and saw.
I whittled it and straightened it, then whittled it some more.
I carved a showy handle, in the shape of swimming fish,
And as I twirled it round and round, I thought it rather swish.

I hunted for some varnish and a set of wooden rasps.
I sanded it and polished it and fitted it with clasps.
I tested it, inspected it, then took it for a tramp.
I stomped for miles on muddy paths in cold and wind and damp.

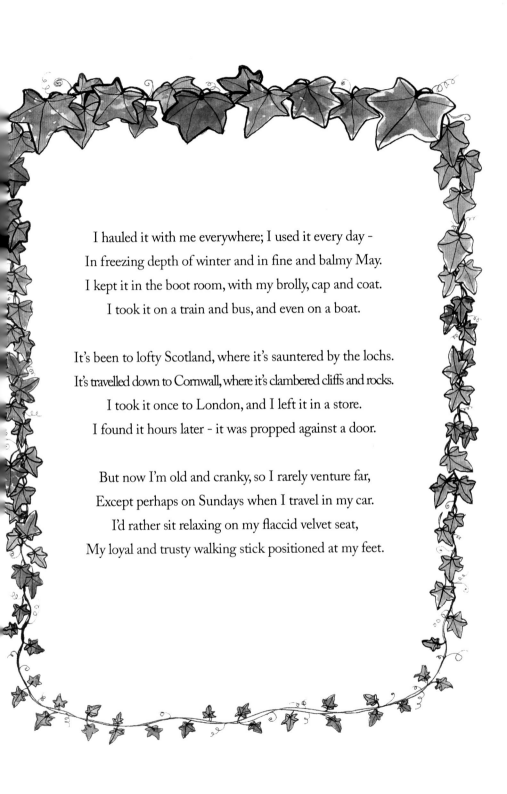

I hauled it with me everywhere; I used it every day -
In freezing depth of winter and in fine and balmy May.
I kept it in the boot room, with my brolly, cap and coat.
I took it on a train and bus, and even on a boat.

It's been to lofty Scotland, where it's sauntered by the lochs.
It's travelled down to Cornwall, where it's clambered cliffs and rocks.
I took it once to London, and I left it in a store.
I found it hours later - it was propped against a door.

But now I'm old and cranky, so I rarely venture far,
Except perhaps on Sundays when I travel in my car.
I'd rather sit relaxing on my flaccid velvet seat,
My loyal and trusty walking stick positioned at my feet.

The Faerie Mountain

Near rugged shores and inky lochs, Schiehallion prevails.
As stronghold of the faeries, she's the guardian of their tales.
And at her foot there is a strath with water through its heart -
An awe-inspiring stimulus for literature and art.

A shroud of grey rests moodily atop her peak of white,
Till stubborn shafts of Highland sun cast rays of welcome light.
Whilst heather clumps in purple waves mid grouse and stags and hares,
An eagle soars above her crown, the carrier of prayers.

Along her burn that gently flows are hammocks, humps and stones -
Decrepit eerie vestiges of ruined Pictish homes.
And to her south there is a glen, deserted, long and low -
A verdant valley, lush and dense, where ferns and flowers grow.

In ancient times, her tranquil glades played host to kings and queens
Who sheltered there from English troops and prayed they'd not be seen.
In later years, a scientist came, enraptured by her form,
And now she's known as Maiden's Pap or sometimes Constant Storm.

'Twas in a distant decade that a lassie went astray -
A girl named Margaret Ritchie left her home and fled away.
The natives duly found her on a raw Schiehallion crest.
They say the faeries took her soul from deep within her breast.

But what of nymphs and pixies, after whom the mount is named?
They're simply comely maidens who appear to laud Beltane.
They dance around the faerie well and drink and sing and cheer,
And in return they boast good health throughout the coming year.

The Artist

He sits aside the craggy rocks
Consuming cans of beer.
A silk bandana round his neck,
A brush behind his ear.

With squinted eye and cigarette,
He starts to sketch the view
Of dusty dunes and coral cliffs,
Beside a sea of blue.

His handsome face is lined and rough;
It's ravaged like the shore.
His nails are grimy, stained with paint,
His calloused fingers sore.

Possessions do not worry him;
He has no need for those.
He owns no car or fancy phone;
He shuns designer clothes.

His hair is oily, long and black;
There's shadow on his chin.
His dark-lashed eyes are big and brown,
Deep-ringed and placed far in.

Upon his back's a baggy shirt,
No longer white or smooth.
He's holes in both his trouser legs,
Whilst cleaves attack his shoes.

No home has he of stone or brick,
No house with stove or bed.
For in a ragged Gypsy van
Is where he lays his head.

The Starling family

Deep within the soffits,
There live three friends of mine.
They gather twigs and bits of wool
And scraps of disused twine.

I hear them in the evening,
As they settle into bed,
For all their fun and frippery
Takes place above my head.

They swoop and glide each morning
And begin amassing tat
To carry to their nesting hole,
A touch of this and that.

Some say that they are scavengers
And wish that they would flee.
They aren't as fair as other birds,
Except, perhaps, to me.

For I think they are clever,
Endearing in their way,
And in my ragged fascia board,
I hope that they will stay.

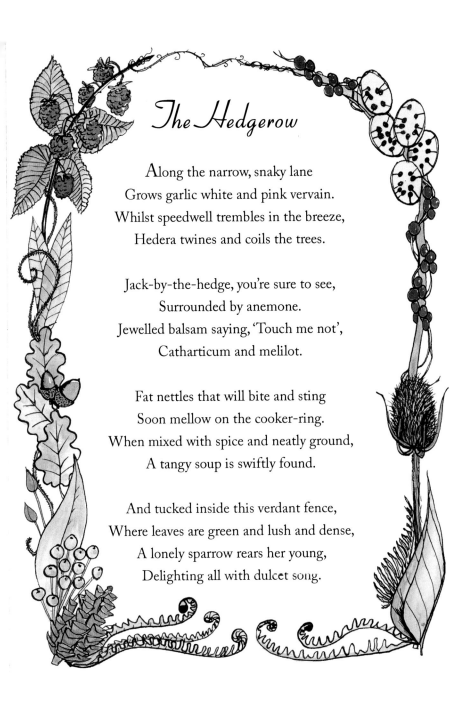

The Hedgerow

Along the narrow, snaky lane
Grows garlic white and pink vervain.
Whilst speedwell trembles in the breeze,
Hedera twines and coils the trees.

Jack-by-the-hedge, you're sure to see,
Surrounded by anemone.
Jewelled balsam saying, 'Touch me not',
Catharticum and melilot.

Fat nettles that will bite and sting
Soon mellow on the cooker-ring.
When mixed with spice and neatly ground,
A tangy soup is swiftly found.

And tucked inside this verdant fence,
Where leaves are green and lush and dense,
A lonely sparrow rears her young,
Delighting all with dulcet song.

The Tooth Fairy

She's a dainty wisp of wonder
And she makes our children smile.
A flimsy, floaty Tinker Bell
Who comes once in a while.

She scatters twinkling sunshine
On the coverlets of the bed.
And places glistering silver coins
Beneath our infant's head.

She's a slice of myth and legend
And her wings are laced with gold.
Her dress is made of filigree;
She's impish and she's bold.

She hovers in the bedroom
When our babes are fast asleep,
And in exchange for jewels and gems,
A tiny tooth she'll keep.

The Hat Stand

A rickety old hat rack,
Stands proudly in the hall,
Bedecked in quirky millinery
That's loved by one and all.

A potpourri of colour,
A diversity of cloth
That's sometimes gnawed and nibbled by
The greedy household moth.

There's Uncle Bertie's bowler
And Katrina's riding hat,
A tattered Tam o' Shanter
Often donned by Grandpa Mac.

A beautiful Balmoral,
A magnificent beret,
A black and white straw boater,
For a picnic in the hay.

A super hero helmet,
For exploring on a bike,
A grubby khaki bucket hat
For taking on a hike.

A fancy fascinator,
For the day the brood are wed,
An Ebenezer sleeping cap
To keep you snug in bed.

But one thing is for certain,
I'm convinced you'll all agree,
If they didn't have a hat rack,
Untidy they would be.

The Seashore

As I stand on the sand beneath watery warmth,
I feel that at last I might breathe.
For the smatter of coastline directly behind
Makes the root of my soul twist and heave.

In a striped knitted hat and a scarf tightly wrapped,
I emerge with a skip to the shore,
Where I forage for winkles, for limpets and wrack
From the minerals, pebbles and ore.

As I squint for a moment and stare at the swell,
I'm aware of a family of seals.
There's a boat in the distance, a dragger perhaps,
Fully loaded with toggles and creels.

When I peer at the seabirds, they squawk and they shriek
As they heartily rummage for worms.
I see curlews and kittiwakes, egrets and shags.
I hear guillemots, whimbrels and terns.

I remain here all morning, absorbing the peace,
With the wavelets engulfing my toes.
I imagine old bottles with messages in
And collect pretty shells to take home.

I return to my boathouse replete and alive,
Overjoyed with my magical finds.
Then I laze in my deckchair and gulp down a drink,
With repose and a sound state of mind.

The Harvest Mouse

She's quick and nimble, brisk, astute,
Concealed in fields of corn.
Her eyesight's poor; her hearing's keen.
She feeds at dusk and dawn.

She's lighter than a two-pence piece;
She's active night and day.
Her softly padded breeding nest
Is shaped from leaves and hay.

She clambers grass and clutches stems,
With tiny grasping toes.
She's dexterous as an acrobat
At glitzy circus shows.

She feasts on berries, seeds and bugs,
And moss and haws and roots.
She nibbles crops and buds and bulbs
And forages new shoots.

She seeks a mate in early May,
Then breeds and spawns and feeds.
She'll nurse her pups for twenty days,
Then cede them when they're weaned.

She lives for barely eighteen months;
Her spell on earth is brief.
And yet a more endearing mouse
You'll surely never meet.

The Ballet Shoes

She only ever wished to dance,
To stand and point with perfect stance.
She'd ask her Ma in humble tone,
"Might I have slippers of my own?"

By age thirteen, she could sauté.
With heels held high, she'd relevé.
But still she had no ballet shoes,
No satin slippers she could use.

She'd dream and wish whilst fast asleep
That borrowed shoes were hers to keep;
She'd hold them in her tiny hands
And think of grand orchestral bands.

She'd practice on her bedroom floor,
Before her mirror, poised and small.
Her dainty arms above her head,
Her tutu stitched with silver thread.

Until, one day, a parcel came
Direct from France in tumbling rain.
The ink was smudged, the script had run,
The wisps of string had come undone.

'Twas from an aunt she'd never met,
A charming lady called Claudette.
And placed within it was a note
That brought a lump into her throat.

'Dear Annalise,' the letter read,
'I found these shoes beneath my bed.
I'm far too old to stun and daze
But if you wear them, you'll amaze!'

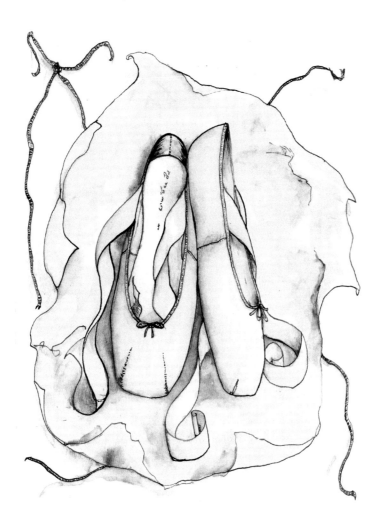

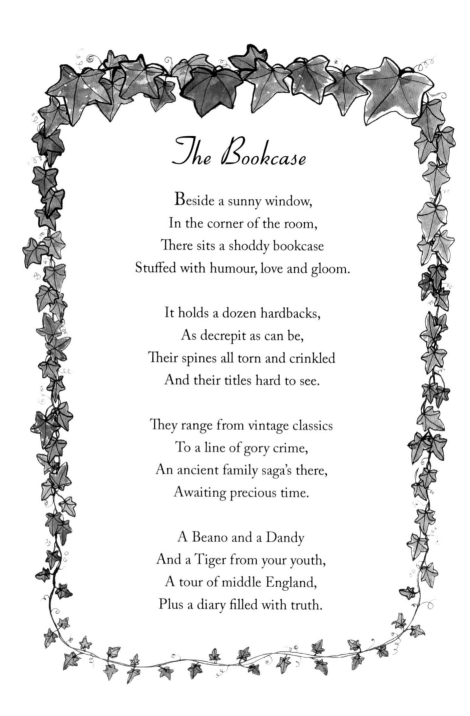

The Bookcase

Beside a sunny window,
In the corner of the room,
There sits a shoddy bookcase
Stuffed with humour, love and gloom.

It holds a dozen hardbacks,
As decrepit as can be,
Their spines all torn and crinkled
And their titles hard to see.

They range from vintage classics
To a line of gory crime,
An ancient family saga's there,
Awaiting precious time.

A Beano and a Dandy
And a Tiger from your youth,
A tour of middle England,
Plus a diary filled with truth.

A pinch of Charlotte Brontë
And some Wilkie Collins too.
A timeless opus that will tell
The tale of Owl and Pooh.

A guide to fancy gardens
And a recipe for bread,
A saucy slice of narrative
To carry up to bed.

And when you think you're past it
And your body's not so pert,
You'll always have a paperback
To keep your mind alert.

Bed

I love to touch my laundered sheet,
So warm and snug about my feet.
I love to sniff my pillow case -
A sweet Gardenia round my face.
And even though my blanket's worn,
It stills and calms me till the morn.

I love to stroke my vintage quilt;
It's patched and hued, and made of silk.
I love my dolly, worse for wear,
That sits beside my teddy bear.
I love my novel, though it's frayed,
My hanky trimmed with lace brocade.

I love my creaky music box,
My dressing gown, my fluffy socks.
I love the portrait on my wall
Of granny in her crocheted shawl.
I love my crackly gramophone,
My blue enamel brush and comb.

I love my tarnished looking-glass -
A bleary relic from my past.
I love the runner on the floor,
The crooked hook upon the door.
I love to sip my morning tea,
Whilst listening to a purling sea.

But most of all, I love my bed -
A peaceful place to rest my head.

The Allotment

There is a patch of land nearby,
That's verdurous, lush and green,
Where faithful natives go to sow
Their brassicas and beans.

They visit daily with their tools -
A shovel and a hoe -
And dig and till and cultivate
So vegetables will grow.

Each plant has been assigned a plot,
With labels bright and clear,
Providing tasty eatables
That sate throughout the year.

A glut of parsnips, chard and peas,
All plentiful and ripe,
As well as swedes and cabbages
And peppers with a stripe.

An obelisk of willow sticks
Stands tall and thin and proud.
Upon it runners, fat and long,
And flowers, gay and loud.

A greenhouse, with some grimy glass,
Sits near the potting shed,
Beside a glut of raspberries
And a vibrant strawberry bed.

Fecund and flush all summer long,
Productive, fruitful, full.
Preserve its goodness while you can
To feed you through the lull.

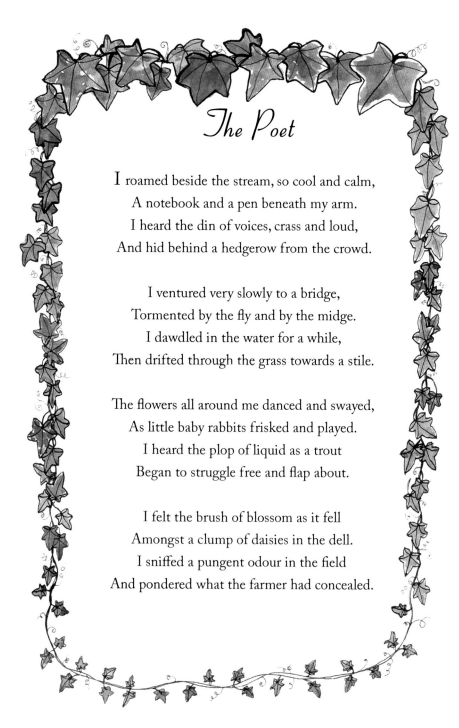

The Poet

I roamed beside the stream, so cool and calm,
A notebook and a pen beneath my arm.
I heard the din of voices, crass and loud,
And hid behind a hedgerow from the crowd.

I ventured very slowly to a bridge,
Tormented by the fly and by the midge.
I dawdled in the water for a while,
Then drifted through the grass towards a stile.

The flowers all around me danced and swayed,
As little baby rabbits frisked and played.
I heard the plop of liquid as a trout
Began to struggle free and flap about.

I felt the brush of blossom as it fell
Amongst a clump of daisies in the dell.
I sniffed a pungent odour in the field
And pondered what the farmer had concealed.

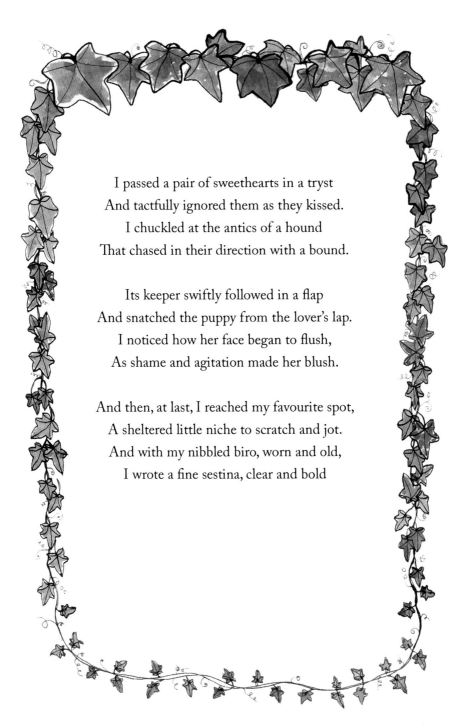

I passed a pair of sweethearts in a tryst
And tactfully ignored them as they kissed.
I chuckled at the antics of a hound
That chased in their direction with a bound.

Its keeper swiftly followed in a flap
And snatched the puppy from the lover's lap.
I noticed how her face began to flush,
As shame and agitation made her blush.

And then, at last, I reached my favourite spot,
A sheltered little niche to scratch and jot.
And with my nibbled biro, worn and old,
I wrote a fine sestina, clear and bold

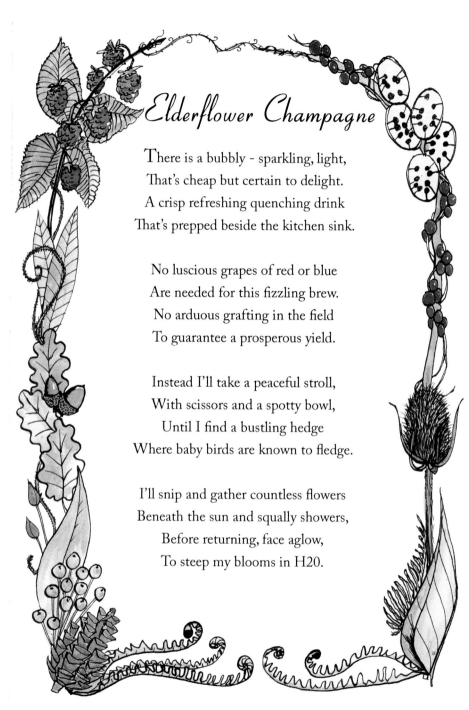

Elderflower Champagne

There is a bubbly - sparkling, light,
That's cheap but certain to delight.
A crisp refreshing quenching drink
That's prepped beside the kitchen sink.

No luscious grapes of red or blue
Are needed for this fizzling brew.
No arduous grafting in the field
To guarantee a prosperous yield.

Instead I'll take a peaceful stroll,
With scissors and a spotty bowl,
Until I find a bustling hedge
Where baby birds are known to fledge.

I'll snip and gather countless flowers
Beneath the sun and squally showers,
Before returning, face aglow,
To steep my blooms in H20.

I'll boost my blend with lemon juice,
Some peel and sugar, then I'll sluice.
I'll add a lid of flimsy weave,
And in the shed, I'll duly leave.

If foam and spume do not appear,
And if the liquid still looks clear,
I'll lift it with a glug of yeast,
A nutrient at very least.

When it froths, I'll drain it off
Through fine and gauzy muslin cloth.
(I should have made a jug or two
To divvy at my barbecue!)

The Picnic

Canapés and fairy cakes, caviar and ham,
Weeny finger sandwiches, replete with raspberry jam.
Pretty Gingham tablecloths are spread upon the grass.
Bollinger and Moët are consumed from crystal glass.

Baskets filled with plates and flasks, with napkins, spoons and forks;
Artful sweethearts hunt out nooks to frolic and disport.
Fancy pots and porringers, a saucer, cup and jug
Sit beside a strawberry sponge, upon the picnic rug.

Lovely, lacy parasols, positioned by the pool,
Are shielding fair and freckled skin and keeping bodies cool.
There's dreamy, drowsy dancing as the band begins to play;
Its tone's as smooth as polished glass and makes you want to sway.

A joint of beef, a roasted duck, some salad and some bread,
A lobster, quail and pheasant pie all make a sumptuous spread.
A game of croquet, cricket, chess or tennis on the court,
Whilst men in boaters smoke cigars and guzzle vintage port.

There's merriment and frippery and flagrant joie de vivre
As tantalising ladies aim to charm and to intrigue.
A patient valet stands and waits to hear his brusque command
As flurried tweenies scurry fast, forever in demand.

Dresses hitched above the knee, whilst splashing in the stream.
Children seek to hook a fish and gobble gooey cream.
Punch and Judy and their stick put on a splendid show.
Debutantes are shy and meek, their faces gleam and glow.

At eventide, a chilly breeze brings goosebumps to the skin.
Blankets, baskets, rugs and chairs are swiftly carried in.
Lovebirds part with weighted hearts, deflated, lorn and lost -
Their passion, thrill and prurience allayed and fleetly quashed.

The Forsaken Garden

Reflecting on my distant past,
I lie and stare through leaded glass.
I see a vista - frowsy, worn,
And all at once I'm lost and lorn.

I think of how the ground once looked,
Its lawns and hedges preened and plucked.
I dream of trysts with handsome lords
Bedecked in doublets, hose and swords.

Awoken from my poignant thoughts,
I rise, befuddled, out of sorts.
I grasp the door and catch my breath.
I seek a gown and start to dress.

Through cobwebs, spiders, dirt and grime,
I leave the house and slowly climb
The mossy steps t'ward broken walls
And old forgotten waterfalls.

I stagger tiredly through the grass
Aside decaying, crumbling paths.
I picture still, their faded grace
And feel a tear upon my face.

I step beneath a grove of trees,
Where fusty smells imbue the breeze.
I spy a craft that's run aground
Beside a lake of filthy brown.

I chance upon my favourite seat,
But as I sit it starts to creak.
It's overrun with weeds and vines
That strangle, stifle and entwine.

I move away with feeble tread,
Until I reach a dingy shed.
Alone and grave, I take a chair
And wish my life would finish there.

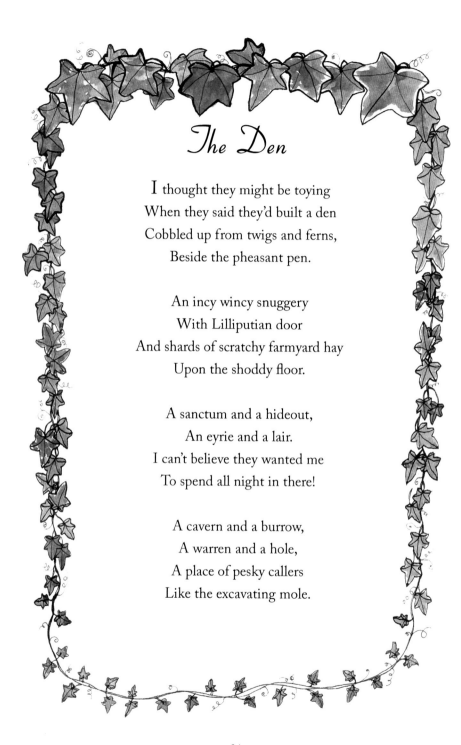

The Den

I thought they might be toying
When they said they'd built a den
Cobbled up from twigs and ferns,
Beside the pheasant pen.

An incy wincy snuggery
With Lilliputian door
And shards of scratchy farmyard hay
Upon the shoddy floor.

A sanctum and a hideout,
An eyrie and a lair.
I can't believe they wanted me
To spend all night in there!

A cavern and a burrow,
A warren and a hole,
A place of pesky callers
Like the excavating mole.

Inside a ring of boulders,
They'll light a blazing fire
To char their foraged edibles
Upon a raging pyre.

Adorned in cosy thermals,
They'll opt to spend the night,
Immured by eerie squeals and squawks,
As woodland owls takes flight.

And when they wake from sleeping,
They'll crave a comfy bed.
I'll find them stiff and grumpy,
With their legs like heavy lead.

But still, they'll have enjoyed it;
It's where they like to be -
That furtive little hidey-hole
That no one else can see.

Love

They say it makes the world revolve,
Dispels our worries, shapes resolve.
It lifts our spirits, high and free,
Gives bliss, delight and comity.

Whilst hatred festers, chaffs and blights,
Devotion cheers and sates and lights;
It carries with it joy and ease,
Composure and the power to please.

It warms the soul and feeds the mind.
It's sympathetic, gentle, kind.
It boosts, inspires, excites, elates,
Supports and binds with staunch embrace.

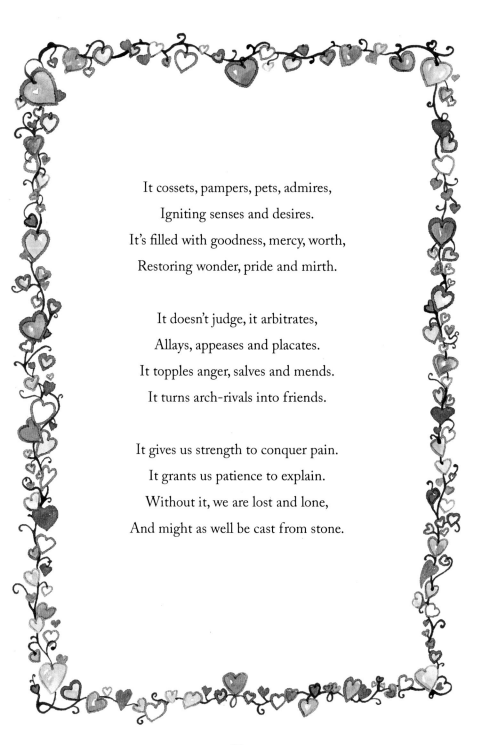

It cossets, pampers, pets, admires,
Igniting senses and desires.
It's filled with goodness, mercy, worth,
Restoring wonder, pride and mirth.

It doesn't judge, it arbitrates,
Allays, appeases and placates.
It topples anger, salves and mends.
It turns arch-rivals into friends.

It gives us strength to conquer pain.
It grants us patience to explain.
Without it, we are lost and lone,
And might as well be cast from stone.

The Castle

Before the moon has left the skies,
In dormant darkness I arise.
I feel a spider brush my head
And spy a beetle in my bed.

I loosen latches, open doors
Which creak and scrape against the floors.
I find a chink and glimpse below;
I see the gate is cloaked in snow.

A shiver runs along my spine,
As down the aisle I hear a whine.
A child's whimper seems so near,
A sacrifice from yesteryear?

I sense a chill from underground.
I'm conscious of a scratching sound;
It could be squirrels, mice or rats,
Starving hounds or feral cats.

The panels and the plundered wings
Play host to ghosts and scary things.
I glimpse a shadow, near the moat
And feel a stricture in my throat.

I'm choking, and I need a drink,
And so I stumble to the sink.
I turn the tap, the water's soiled.
My stomach spins; it churns and roils.

I risk a swig - it tastes of bog,
Of swamp and mud, morass and quag.
I start to vomit and to shake;
I'm desperate for a swift escape.

And so I head towards the crypt,
On rugs and runners, frayed and ripped.
And laced with boldness, nerve and gall,
I vanish though the castle wall.

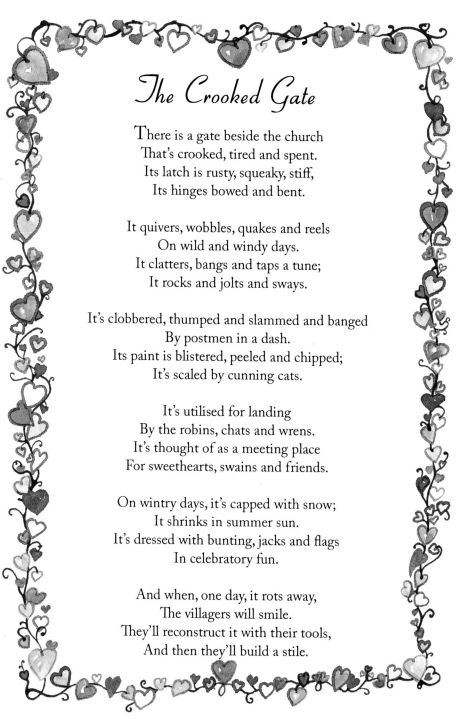

The Crooked Gate

There is a gate beside the church
That's crooked, tired and spent.
Its latch is rusty, squeaky, stiff,
Its hinges bowed and bent.

It quivers, wobbles, quakes and reels
On wild and windy days.
It clatters, bangs and taps a tune;
It rocks and jolts and sways.

It's clobbered, thumped and slammed and banged
By postmen in a dash.
Its paint is blistered, peeled and chipped;
It's scaled by cunning cats.

It's utilised for landing
By the robins, chats and wrens.
It's thought of as a meeting place
For sweethearts, swains and friends.

On wintry days, it's capped with snow;
It shrinks in summer sun.
It's dressed with bunting, jacks and flags
In celebratory fun.

And when, one day, it rots away,
The villagers will smile.
They'll reconstruct it with their tools,
And then they'll build a stile.

The Ice Skater

When days are short and warmth is sparse,
I wake with joy and glee;
For scorching summer sunshine is
Anathema to me.

Bedecked in woollens, hued and warm,
I trudge towards the lake,
And with my boots laced firm and tight,
I swiftly start to skate.

I swirl and twirl and zwer and whirl,
As carefree as can be,
Admiring icy chandeliers,
Which hang from every tree.

I spin, gyrate; I twist, rotate,
Till dizzy I become.
I laugh and shout and lark about
Beneath the winter sun.

I slide and glide with grace and pride,
Enlivened, spurred and spry.
I'm brisk and light and full of zip;
I feel like I could fly!

And there I stay, content to play,
Alone, at ease and free.
Until some noisy revellers
Invade my privacy.

Wellies

On talcum-powdered hilltops
And in sticky, sloppy mud,
They'll keep you dry and cosy,
Take you splashing in a flood.

They come in different sizes,
And they're lined with downy fluff.
They're either pretty snazzy
Or they're grubby, smutched and rough.

I own some that are spotty,
And I own some that are smart.
I have a pair for festivals,
Bedecked in purple hearts.

A pair dwells in my garden,
And I've crammed them full of blooms.
I even have some yellow ones
Adorned in red balloons.

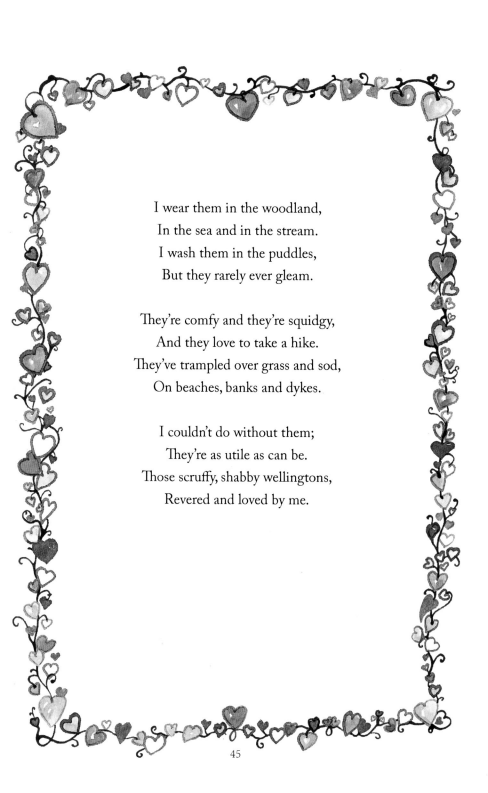

I wear them in the woodland,
In the sea and in the stream.
I wash them in the puddles,
But they rarely ever gleam.

They're comfy and they're squidgy,
And they love to take a hike.
They've trampled over grass and sod,
On beaches, banks and dykes.

I couldn't do without them;
They're as utile as can be.
Those scruffy, shabby wellingtons,
Revered and loved by me.

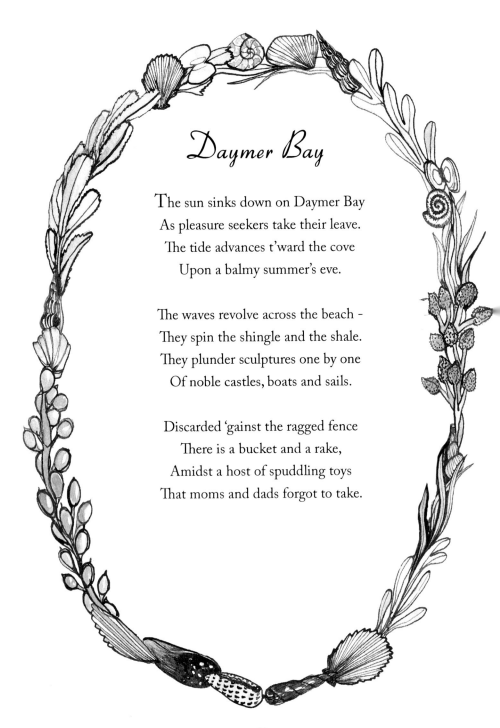

Daymer Bay

The sun sinks down on Daymer Bay
As pleasure seekers take their leave.
The tide advances t'ward the cove
Upon a balmy summer's eve.

The waves revolve across the beach -
They spin the shingle and the shale.
They plunder sculptures one by one
Of noble castles, boats and sails.

Discarded 'gainst the ragged fence
There is a bucket and a rake,
Amidst a host of spuddling toys
That moms and dads forgot to take.

Beside the dunes is Enodoc:
Basilica of peace and rest,
Where lies a poet laureate,
In sacred ground, revered and blessed.

A little stroll finds Stepper Point,
A knoll to conquer, low but steep,
Deserted now this eventide,
To let the dragon softly sleep.

And tucked behind a jagged rock,
A lonesome surfer sits and waits,
For early evening out at sea,
Is when and where his stunts take place.

Nettle Soup

First you don your wellies,
And then you find a glove.
You meander to the greenhouse,
With your trusty garden trug.

You trample through the brambles,
Being careful not to fall.
You find a patch of nettles,
Then you hold on tight and pull.

You take them to the kitchen,
And you blanch them in a pot.
You fry some onion in a pan
And add some tasty stock.

You chop some juicy carrots,
And some celery and bay,
Then add a leek and lemon juice
And fuse with herb bouquet.

Now tip in wilted nettles
And take a little sip.
Lift the pot towards the sink -
Be mindful not to trip.

Liquidize your edibles,
And add a swirl of cream.
Then sprinkle pepper, salt and mint…
Your soup is vibrant green!

The Kingfisher

Mid lichen-covered branches,
Beside the river deep,
I saw a flash of colour,
And so to the bank did creep.

I wandered circumspectly,
To where the flash had been,
And crouched amid the verdure;
It was clammy, dank and green.

At once he did appear there,
A blaze of blaring blue.
And from his haughty countenance
I guessed he'd seen me too.

His beak was stretched and pointed
And his amber breast aglow.
His movement, once so rapid,
Seemed phlegmatic, slack and slow.

He sat composed and silent,
Eyeballs flitting here and there.
So cunning and intelligent,
Concealed within his lair.

And then at last he glimpsed it,
His unsuspecting prey,
And plunged into the watercourse
To carry it away.

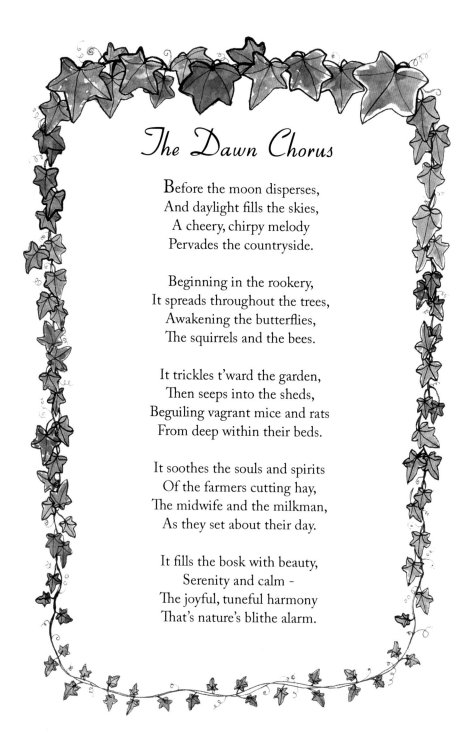

The Dawn Chorus

Before the moon disperses,
And daylight fills the skies,
A cheery, chirpy melody
Pervades the countryside.

Beginning in the rookery,
It spreads throughout the trees,
Awakening the butterflies,
The squirrels and the bees.

It trickles t'ward the garden,
Then seeps into the sheds,
Beguiling vagrant mice and rats
From deep within their beds.

It soothes the souls and spirits
Of the farmers cutting hay,
The midwife and the milkman,
As they set about their day.

It fills the bosk with beauty,
Serenity and calm -
The joyful, tuneful harmony
That's nature's blithe alarm.

The She-Cat

She's eyes that shine like malachite -
Pellucid pools of green.
She's paws as soft as goslings' wings.
How does she keep them clean?

She's agile and she's graceful,
But as fractious as can be.
She leaps and bounces, captures prey
And scales the tallest tree.

She's really rather canny,
And I've known her to be shrewd.
She's elegant and dignified,
Ne'er blundering or crude.

She's sometimes quite affectionate,
But more than often not.
It usually depends upon
What's lurking in her pot.

She's arrogant, self-confident,
Presumptuous, proud and cool.
She's Empress of her bailiwick,
A creature born to rule.

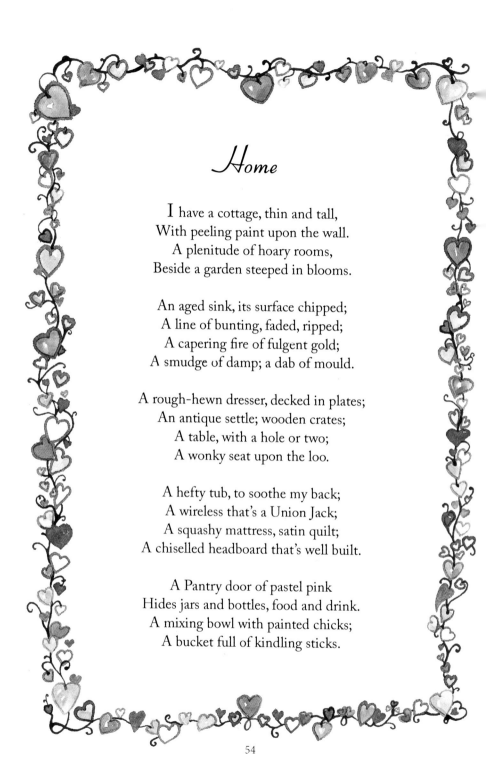

Home

I have a cottage, thin and tall,
With peeling paint upon the wall.
A plenitude of hoary rooms,
Beside a garden steeped in blooms.

An aged sink, its surface chipped;
A line of bunting, faded, ripped;
A capering fire of fulgent gold;
A smudge of damp; a dab of mould.

A rough-hewn dresser, decked in plates;
An antique settle; wooden crates;
A table, with a hole or two;
A wonky seat upon the loo.

A hefty tub, to soothe my back;
A wireless that's a Union Jack;
A squashy mattress, satin quilt;
A chiselled headboard that's well built.

A Pantry door of pastel pink
Hides jars and bottles, food and drink.
A mixing bowl with painted chicks;
A bucket full of kindling sticks.

A statue with a torn straw hat;
An old church pew, a dozing cat;
A willow wigwam, peas and beans;
A deckchair, splitting at the seams.

A glut of buxus, clipped and shaped;
Some linen curtains loosely draped;
A floorboard, which will reel and rock,
Beneath a German cuckoo clock.

Some incense and an oil lamp too;
Some Pukka tea, to meld a brew;
A brimming bookshelf, stacked with tat;
A hardback classic, bent and cracked.

My home is rustic, verdant, lush.
It's cushy, quirky, spared from rush.
It's timeless and it's fancy-free -
The perfect place for me to be!

Herbs and Spices

Chilli, rosemary, dill and mint.
Ginger spice to fire your drink.
Salt and pepper, sage and mace.
Aloe Vera for your face.

Basil, lemon, spearmint, thyme,
Woody sorrel, fragrant lime.
Subtle saffron, pale and gold.
Oregano, fresh and bold.

For your curry, fennel seed.
Soothe your ache with malva weed.
Marjoram, to help your feet.
Chamomile, for restful sleep.

Eucalyptus lets you breathe,
Catnip comforts when you teethe.
Jasmine's there to hoist your mood.
Dulse adds goodness to your food.

Should you wish to shed some weight,
Black-eyed pea tastes really great.
Should you want to quell the croup,
Bearberry tea and garlic soup.

And when your joints begin to sing,
Devil's claw is just the thing.
Smear it on both morn and night,
And in a week you'll feel all right.

Herbs and spices, wholesome, good.
Grown in gardens, and in woods.
Utilise them while you can,
To keep your body spick and span.

The Bird Table

You'll place it near your window,
Betwixt the flowers and weeds.
And laden it with nuts and bread
And multicoloured seeds.

You'll build a ledge for chatter,
And a plank for idle play.
You'll forge a roof from wood and sticks,
To keep the rain away.

Abundant entertainment,
You'll find it will provide.
Whilst washing up or baking buns,
Your gaze will drift outside.

You'll marvel at the swiftness,
The agility and speed,
Of all the dainty garden birds
That land to filch their feed.

And when the table's empty,
Its inhabitants at rest,
The sneaky squirrel will appear
To pilfer and ingest.

The Seal Trip

Whilst seeking seals with Callum Brown,
We spied a buccaneer.
So, with the throttle buried deep,
We sped across the mere.

Our rusty vessel rocked and jarred;
It lurched in swells of white.
But still we ventured on and on
To triumph in our plight.

We surged across the navy loch,
Inhaling noxious fumes,
Wrapped tight against the Highland wind,
With nothing to consume

Except a shelf of finest malt,
Which trembled in the haste,
As Callum veered aside the rocks
With piety and pace.

His face was red with ire and rage;
His fist was clenched and clasped.
But as we landed by the beach,
He simply stood and gasped.

Before us was a man in tweeds,
No poacher, thief or crook.
"Och heck," he said, with cheeks ablush,
"Ah main hae bin mistook!"

The Highland Fisherman

Amidst the hefty upland hills
Live honest folk with ancient skills:
The cooper and the lowly boots,
The man who heads the pheasant shoots.

The fisher in his humble shack
Is known to all as 'Trawler Jack'.
He rises early every day,
To keep his fiery bride at bay.

At dusky dawn, he finds a spot
To sail his raft into the loch,
But as the hours slowly pass,
He sees no salmon, pike or bass.

Alas, the seal, so apt and deft;
He's poached the fish and swiftly left.
The poor old fisher's all alone,
With not a jot to ferry home.

As mist descends, Jack leaves his boat;
It sways and bounces, bobs afloat.
No catch has he within his grasp.
He dreads the questions he'll be asked.

He travels homeward, cold and wet,
And at the door he's swiftly met.
He sighs and pats his faithful dog.
His wife stands looming, like the fog.

"Hoo mony hae ye caught?" she shouts,
But Jack just shrugs and starts to pout.
"Then it's mince and tatties fur yer tea,
Nae cullen skink fur me an ye!"

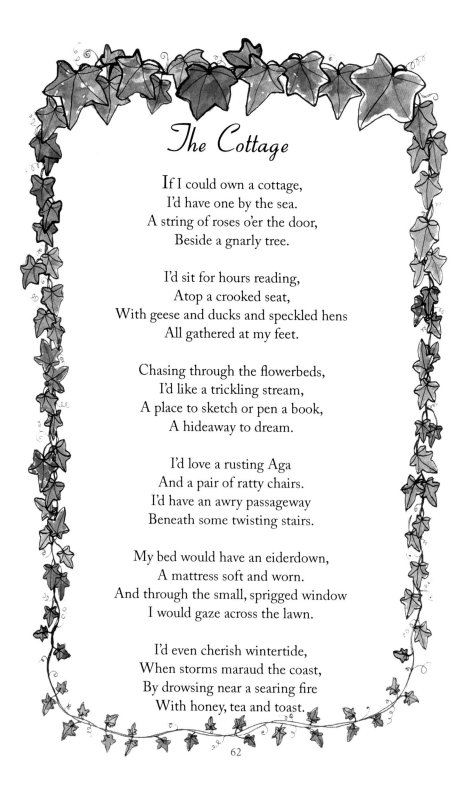

The Cottage

If I could own a cottage,
I'd have one by the sea.
A string of roses o'er the door,
Beside a gnarly tree.

I'd sit for hours reading,
Atop a crooked seat,
With geese and ducks and speckled hens
All gathered at my feet.

Chasing through the flowerbeds,
I'd like a trickling stream,
A place to sketch or pen a book,
A hideaway to dream.

I'd love a rusting Aga
And a pair of ratty chairs.
I'd have an awry passageway
Beneath some twisting stairs.

My bed would have an eiderdown,
A mattress soft and worn.
And through the small, sprigged window
I would gaze across the lawn.

I'd even cherish wintertide,
When storms maraud the coast,
By drowsing near a searing fire
With honey, tea and toast.

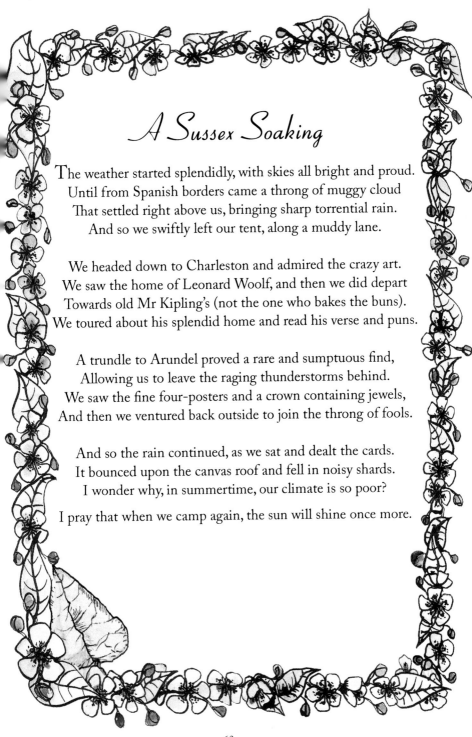

A Sussex Soaking

The weather started splendidly, with skies all bright and proud.
Until from Spanish borders came a throng of muggy cloud
That settled right above us, bringing sharp torrential rain.
And so we swiftly left our tent, along a muddy lane.

We headed down to Charleston and admired the crazy art.
We saw the home of Leonard Woolf, and then we did depart
Towards old Mr Kipling's (not the one who bakes the buns).
We toured about his splendid home and read his verse and puns.

A trundle to Arundel proved a rare and sumptuous find,
Allowing us to leave the raging thunderstorms behind.
We saw the fine four-posters and a crown containing jewels,
And then we ventured back outside to join the throng of fools.

And so the rain continued, as we sat and dealt the cards.
It bounced upon the canvas roof and fell in noisy shards.
I wonder why, in summertime, our climate is so poor?

I pray that when we camp again, the sun will shine once more.

The Horseshoe Pool

I sometimes stroll beside the pool
Where once, when young and trim,
I let the water beckon me
To paddle, float and swim.

I ponder hot and limpid days,
'Neath crests of beryl blue,
Cavorting on the soggy bank
With little else to do...

My dress abandoned on the grass,
Beside a wooden shack;
A rowing boat that lightly jounced
Upon a stolid lap;

The squelch of mud betwixt my toes;
A chronic buzz of pests;
A gallant dive, with breath held tight
And legs against my chest;

The swoosh of leaves that rocked and swayed
And quivered in the sky,
Enchanting and bewitching me,
Whilst on my back I'd lie;

The calling of the nightingale,
The cuckoo and the thrush;
The peace and sheer placidity,
Away from stress and rush.

Then in a burst, abrupt and brisk,
My wistful daydream ends.
For standing, calling out to me,
Are three of my best friends.

The Happy Campers

A furtive clearing by the rocks
Will be your wildest dream.
Together with a campfire
And an easygoing stream.

A site of contemplation,
Where serenity is found.
A little shelter by the sea,
Where infants splash around.

You'll hear the pulse of tapping
As you start to plot and pitch,
Creating an Arcadia
To charm and to bewitch.

You'll dangle pastel garlands
And a lantern from the trees.
And then you'll hang a hammock
Midst the butterflies and bees.

You'll dread the clout of footballs,
As the children frisk and play,
Disrupting your tranquillity
With din and disarray.

And later you will giggle,
As the gin begins to flow.
(You'll suffer in the morning
When the cockerel starts to crow.)

You'll loathe the frenzied bustle
Of the early bathroom rush.
You'll wish you'd risen early
To avoid the crazy crush.

But when the week is over
And equipment's stored away,
You'll feel refreshed and livened by
Your camping holiday.

The Faerie Glen

I crossed a bridge where toadstools grow,
Atop a river's gentle flow.
I climbed down stairs that arced and wound,
Until I reached the hallowed ground.

The roots beneath me tangled tight,
To keep the pixies out of sight,
To hide the faeries, sprites and elves
And keep them safe from wicked spells.

I lounged beside a deep ravine,
Encased by banks of velvet green.
And there I heard the waters splash:
A deafening, lunging, slamming crash.

The mossy crags felt cold and damp,
And lichen grew on every bank.
A skein of cobwebs clutched the trees,
Ensconced and sheltered from the breeze.

I saw an otter dive and dip,
His snakelike body roll and flip.
I paused in silence, held my stance
To watch him frolic, lark and dance.

I wound my way through ancient wood,
Where golden beeches long have stood
Until I found a secret nook -
A place to settle with my book.

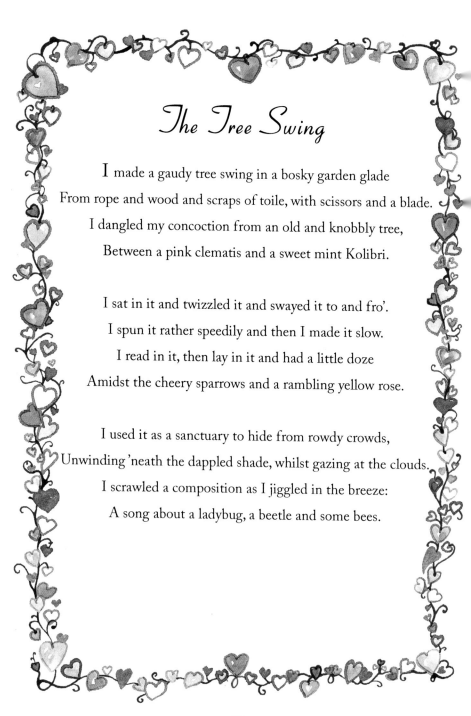

The Tree Swing

I made a gaudy tree swing in a bosky garden glade
From rope and wood and scraps of toile, with scissors and a blade.
I dangled my concoction from an old and knobbly tree,
Between a pink clematis and a sweet mint Kolibri.

I sat in it and twizzled it and swayed it to and fro'.
I spun it rather speedily and then I made it slow.
I read in it, then lay in it and had a little doze
Amidst the cheery sparrows and a rambling yellow rose.

I used it as a sanctuary to hide from rowdy crowds,
Unwinding 'neath the dappled shade, whilst gazing at the clouds.
I scrawled a composition as I jiggled in the breeze:
A song about a ladybug, a beetle and some bees.

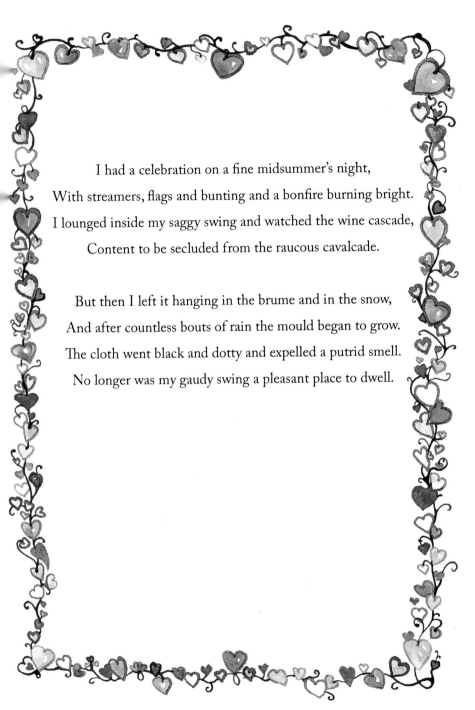

I had a celebration on a fine midsummer's night,
With streamers, flags and bunting and a bonfire burning bright.
I lounged inside my saggy swing and watched the wine cascade,
Content to be secluded from the raucous cavalcade.

But then I left it hanging in the brume and in the snow,
And after countless bouts of rain the mould began to grow.
The cloth went black and dotty and expelled a putrid smell.
No longer was my gaudy swing a pleasant place to dwell.

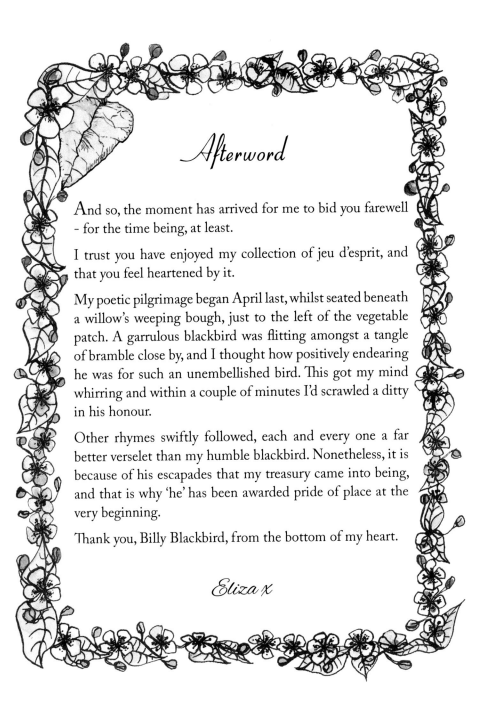

Afterword

And so, the moment has arrived for me to bid you farewell - for the time being, at least.

I trust you have enjoyed my collection of jeu d'esprit, and that you feel heartened by it.

My poetic pilgrimage began April last, whilst seated beneath a willow's weeping bough, just to the left of the vegetable patch. A garrulous blackbird was flitting amongst a tangle of bramble close by, and I thought how positively endearing he was for such an unembellished bird. This got my mind whirring and within a couple of minutes I'd scrawled a ditty in his honour.

Other rhymes swiftly followed, each and every one a far better verselet than my humble blackbird. Nonetheless, it is because of his escapades that my treasury came into being, and that is why 'he' has been awarded pride of place at the very beginning.

Thank you, Billy Blackbird, from the bottom of my heart.

Eliza x

Acknowledgments

Enormous thanks are due to many people - in particular, my long-suffering husband, David and my beautiful son, Henry, whose patience, support and encouragement have been boundless. You are wonderful, both of you, and without your assistance I wouldn't have any adventures to write about!

I give heartfelt gratitude to everyone at High Town Writers, especially Sam for our lovely lengthy lunches and literary chit-chat, and to Alex for his wordsmithery and meticulous attention to detail.

I also thank Delphine for her incredible illustrations, and Chella at Honeybee Books for piecing words and pictures together to make such an eye-catching anthology.

And, last but not least, I am indebted, as ever, to my dependable parents who are always there just when I need them.

About the Author

Elizabeth Henry, self-confessed romanticist and bibliophile writes......

'My infatuation with books began at a very early age. I grew up in a house surrounded by them, and I loved to escape inside stories about 'The Four Marys', 'Winnie the Pooh' and 'Jemima Puddle-Duck'. I yearned incessantly to have magical adventures with Enid Blyton's fairy folk and to clamber through a wardrobe or a looking glass to a make-believe world.

As I matured, I moved on to the classics, in particular the Brontës and Dickens, but now my taste has broadened, and as long as I can lose myself within the pages of a well-thumbed epic, I am content.

In recent times, I have discovered a partiality for poetry, which, oddly enough, stemmed from the accidental finding of a jaunty little jingle by Rudyard Kipling. It was called 'The Bee-Boy's Song' and was featured in a novel by my favourite author. This droll and delightful ditty spurred me to buy a book of verse, which I found surprisingly enlightening, and a few months on, following a brief encounter with a bird, I began writing my own. I am now a member of The Society of Classical Poets.

As well as a fondness for literature, I am also passionate about ancient castles, hoary historic houses and the wild and wonderful landscape which begirds me. I love nature and have an unquenchable thirst for travel—particularly round Scotland and Wales; they are awe-inspiring and never fail to fuel my passion to write.

My home is a charming but slightly ramshackle cottage in Shropshire, where I live with my horticulturalist husband and my eight-year-old son. In our vast and verdurous garden, we grow blowsy blooms and wholesome vegetables; we also keep five colourful chickens for eggs. We have oodles of adventures together, many of which are fantastical enough to write about… And so I do!'